Testimonials

I don't want to live in fear or feel like a prisoner in my own home. Women's Personal Safety 101 gives me the power and it feels good being in charge.
- *Andrea Roane, News Anchor WUSA 9*
  Washington, DC

At a time when statistics speak to the rising number of women who are beaten, robbed, raped, assaulted and even murdered every hour of the day, this book is a powerful and useful tool that every woman must read, study, and learn. Women's Personal Safety 101 is not only a how-to book, it's also filled with telephone numbers and website information to help women who find themselves in harm's way.
- *Renee J. Nash, Director of Information and Public Affairs*
  Executive Producer of Tony Is Taking It to the Streets on the Steve Harvey Morning Show
  Executive Producer of the Sighlent Storm on WHUR-WORLD 96.3HD2
  WHUR 96.3FM - Washington

This book covers so many aspects on women's personal safety as well as it is a great read and no other book offers the professional advice, friendly support, and in-depth help with Women's Personal Safety.
- *Robin Gibson, Black Enterprise*
  Director of Multi-Media Sales

Women's Personal Safety 101 is a riveting systematic guide to personal safety. Samuel Scott's book outlines what to be on the lookout for from potential predators and how to most effectively defend yourself in an emergency. This book is a must read for all women as it outlines safety precautions to prevent an attack and provides self-defense techniques to utilize in the event of an attack. Women's Personal Safety 101 shines above the rest amongst personal safety guides! To use the old adage: An ounce of prevention is worth a pound of cure, so please take the time to read this most important book!
- *Dr. Janice P. Hay, Elementary School Principal*
  Prince George's County Maryland Public Schools

Deeply insightful......Master Scott is uniquely qualified to have written this book. As a former Correction's Officer, he's actually been "inside the mind" of the predator, and understands what makes them tick, how they choose a victim, and more importantly, what makes them AVOID some potential targets! Armed with this deep insight, you can tip the scales in your favor to reduce the chances of being the "next" victim. Great work Master Scott! This should be MANDATORY reading for every woman.
　　　　- Toby Milroy, Chief Operating Office,
　　　　NAPMA(National Association of Professional Martial Artists)

Master Scott's book is an easy read for communities and organizations to use for the support of women. On behalf of all husbands, fathers and brothers who want an avenue to protect their wives, daughters or sisters, Master Scott gives them an avenue to be self-aware.
　　　　- Mayor Darrell A. Miller, Town of Capitol Heights, MD

The book is ideal for the woman who wants to learn basic survival techniques and be proactive about her own safety. I just wish I had studied these techniques years ago, especially while in college. Many young women are assaulted while on campus by the "predators" that Sam Scott so vividly describes. This is a "must read" for both young woman and young men as they venture out into the world we live in today.
　　　　- Denise Benhoff, MA, Dynamic Choices
　　　　Training Specialist & Consultant

This book is a simple to read personal safety resource designed to empower women to protect themselves against today's violent predators.
　　　　- James T. Overton, Chief of Police / Assoc.
　　　　VP for Public Safety, Delaware State University

I think Samuel Scott's Book "Women's Personal Safety 101" is an essential and must read book for any woman or child. As a woman and mother of two young daughters, learning how to protect myself and them from predators is crucial and not knowing can be detrimental."
　　　　- Johnetta Hardy, Author, Entrepreneur Professor, and Entrepreneur
　　　　Director at Howard University

WOMEN'S PERSONAL SAFETY 101

"It's not, if you'll need it, but when you'll need it!"
Be prepared!

--- Samuel Scott

Order this book online at www.trafford.com
or email orders@trafford.com

Most Trafford titles are also available at major online book retailers.

Joyce Steele: Final Editor

Models: Charles Brown, Jeremy Brown, Andy Butts, Cynthia "Ayedeli" Edwards, Rhonda Ferrell,
Carey Gormes, Jung Yeon Kim, Cydney McCurdy, Nia Mitchell, Brian Nutter, Bobby Perry,
Valencia Robinson, Emily Roos, Jerrell Scott, Ernesto Toppin, Brian Williams, Johanna Williams

Printed in Victoria, BC, Canada.

ISBN: 9781425163198 (sc)
ISBN: 9781425163204 (e)

*Our mission is to efficiently provide the world's finest, most comprehensive book publishing
service, enabling every author to experience success. To find out how to publish your book,
your way, and have it available worldwide, visit us online at www.trafford.com*

Trafford rev. 11/12/2009

www.trafford.com

North America & international
toll-free: 1 888 232 4444 (USA & Canada)
phone: 250 383 6864 ♦ fax: 812 355 4082

Dedication

To my Mother:

I would like to dedicate this book to my loving mother, the late Thelma Mae Scott, who I call my Master Teacher.

Thank you for giving me a strong foundation from which to grow in the spirit of love and compassion for all. I will share your words of encouragement, compassion and love for one another to all who will listen.

Lastly, I will continue to be an instrument for the Creator to use to help bring about positive change in this world.

To my children, Jerrell and Indya Scott:

Let this book be a small testimony that all things are possible... if you just believe!

CONTENTS

Techniques:

- *Stun and escape*

- *Kicks*

- *Strikes*

- *Stances*

- *Avoiding a Strike*

- *How to fall properly*

- *Quick releases from wrist and arm grabs*

- *Chokehold escapes*

- *Defense from the ground*

- *Rape defense*

- *How to use everyday items as a weapon*

- *The keychain weapon*

Acknowledgements

First and foremost I would like to give thanks to the Creator for his guidance and depositing in me the right spirit to help make a difference.

Next, I would like to thank my partner and friend, Master Wallace Powell for his undying support and encouragement; my staff and students for believing in my vision; my elite group of black belts (Shi fu Darryl Player, Shi fu Nia Mitchell, Shi fu JT Bowers, Shi fu Kim Dominguez, Shi fu Al Stevenson, Shi fu Jerrell Scott, Shi fu Jerome Dookie, Shi fu Al Davis, Guro Chuck Brown, Guro Carey Gormes, Guro Bobby Perry, Guro Rhonda Ferrell and Guro Valencia Robinson) who help me on a daily basis share the transformational powers of martial arts.

Last, but surely not least, I would like to give a very special thanks to Guro Rhonda Ferrell, Guro Valencia Robinson, as well as Guro Brian Williams and Guro Johanna Williams for helping keep the Full Circle Family together and traveling with me to help spread the word to thousands of women about personal safety. Their commitment and desire to empower women through our national "Women's Personal Safety Program" has been the air under my wings...and for that I am truly grateful.

Note from the Author

This simple to read book was born out of my desire to help women learn how to effectively protect themselves against today's vicious predators.

As a 15-year veteran of Prince George's County Maryland Department of Corrections, I had the opportunity to sit face-to-face with the predator and gained a better understanding of what they look for in their victims.

When you read this book you will learn how simple it really is to avoid fitting what is known as the "Victim Profile". However, it will be up to you to act on what you've learned. Gaining knowledge about a subject as important as this and not taking action is similar to inviting the predator into your home!

Read…. Then act!!

"You only get one shot at life. This is not a dress rehearsal."

Letter from the Predator

Greetings! Allow me to introduce myself. I am your absolute worst nightmare. I am the one that hunts you down like an animal stalking his prey. Everyday I watch the way you walk, talk, move and yes, I even watch how you sleep. Most of the time I approach you and ask you a question. The way you answer greatly impacts my decision in whether to make you my next victim. I must admit, most of you make my work too easy - leaving your windows and curtains open in your homes and patio doors unlocked. You shop and travel alone at night, totally unaware of the fact that I am following you because you're too busy talking on your cell phone.

Some of you, in your desire to find a mate, stay out late in clubs, where I observe you, offer you a drink laced with my odorless date rape drug or simply follow you home so that I can invite you into your own home.

It still amazes me how easy it is to get you to chat with me online where I tell you everything you want to hear until you let down what little guard you have left. Then I simply work my way into your home and rape you.

As I said, I am your worst nightmare, and as long as you continue to be blind to the reality of who I am, you will continue to be my victim.

Always,
the Predator

This letter is a compilation of answers I received when I asked a number of criminals the question, "What's the number one reason you choose a certain victim?" The overwhelming response was "their total lack of awareness!"

Chapter 1: The Predator

During my 15 years as a Corrections Officer, I had the opportunity to sit face-to-face with many criminals who openly shared their stories with me. While some of them agreed to do this as a way of helping my cause, others were just excited to talk about their craft. When I asked them why they chose a life of crime, the answer was pretty consistent, especially with the younger criminals. Most of them stated that no one really cared about them; they grew up in a dysfunctional family where domestic violence, drugs and poverty permeated their childhood experience. Others, who came from good, stable families, allowed the magnetic attraction of peer pressure to steer them toward the wrong crowd, into gang activity and drug dealing.

We've all heard the unfortunate stories about the pro athletes who got caught up in drugs, the 'A' student that shoots another person to fit in with the cool crowd, or the church boy who goes to church with his parents every Sunday and the rest of the week sells death (drugs) on the streets, destroying the few communities we have left.

There are also the hardened career criminals, who made a decision early in life that they were going to live the life of crime and basically take whatever it was they wanted, be it money, property, or sex. I call them the angry criminal because they blamed society or the system for not providing them an "equal opportunity" to become productive citizens.

However, when I honed in on the sexual predators, their reasoning was somewhat different:

- Most stated that they were either molested as a child, or grew up in an environment where sexual abuse was prevalent.

- Some were angry with women in general, blaming them for most of their troubles. They spoke about relationships that went sour, a wife running off with their best friend, or catching their significant other in a compromising situation. I could see fire in their eyes as they replayed the event in their mind. They appeared to have lost all respect for women and had no remorse whatsoever. Most of them had either brutally beaten or killed their victims.

- Then you have the serial rapists that appeared to be obsessed with sex, the power they possessed over their victims and for some, the fame of being on television.

In any event, all of the criminals that I have either sat face to face with, or researched and studied over the years, seemed to have a particular pattern or system that they followed in selecting their victim. Although there were some cases of random attacks, most of them would observe their victim from a distance to see if they appeared to be aware of their surroundings. They would observe their body language to pick up on certain cues. Next, they would approach them and put them through what is called the "interview". The way this works is, they approach their potential victim and ask them a question such as, "Do you have the time?" Their response and body language determined whether or not they would be selected as the next victim.

Now, think back for a second. How many times has a stranger asked you for directions, the time, a cigarette, a light or anything that allowed him to observe your reaction? Now granted, some of these questions could have been legitimate; however, if you know this is one of the methods the predator uses to choose his victims, why take the chance?

Most predators seek the path of least resistance by looking for:

- Someone who appears weak, timid, or shy.

- Someone who's unaware of their surroundings.

- Someone who uses poor judgment, like shopping alone at night or walking to their vehicle with both hands full.

- Areas (ambush zones) that are conducive for an attack.

- A quick escape route.

Steps to take to avoid fitting the victim profile:

- Walk with a sense of purpose and confidence.

- Display good posture; stand straight with your shoulders back.

- Scan and observe your surroundings.

- Have your purse over your right shoulder and pulled slightly to the front.

- Stay off your cell phone while shopping or wait until you're in an area where you can either sit or stand with your back against a wall.

If approached by a stranger:

- Step back and to the side with one foot and assume what I call the "interview stance" (See Interview stance on page 94).

- Respond to the person in a calm but authoritative manner, "Can I help you sir?!"

- Look him in the eyes, and then scan him up and down as if taking a snapshot.

- If he asks a question, for example, "Do you have the time?", keep your hands at eye level, flip your wrist up, tell him the time, and continue to observe him as he walks away (do not look down at your watch).

- If you sense something is wrong, leave the area right away. Find a security officer and ask to be escorted to your vehicle.

By responding in this manner, you are communicating to the predator that you are fully aware and alert to the interview process and are prepared to defend yourself.

Chapter 2: Awareness

Awareness is a critical component of personal safety. It is your first line of defense in avoiding an attack or a potentially unsafe environment.

It's also important to know that, along with awareness, you need to have good assessment skills. This will allow you to observe someone or something and quickly determine whether or not a threat is present so that you can take the appropriate action.

As a personal safety advisor, I spend a few hours a week checking to see if women that are out shopping are exercising good awareness skills. I start at department stores or mall parking lots and sit and observe their behavior. While some have very good awareness practices, most are literally walking targets. Below are some of my observations:

- Carrying bags in both hands.

- Walking straight up to their vehicle without checking in, under or around it.

- Digging in their purse, while at the car with their back turned, looking for their car keys.

- Talking on their cell phone without having a clue as to what is going on around them.

- While in the parking lot, I open my tailgate/trunk, and stand there as though I am looking for something in my trunk. Eight out of ten women routinely walk within arms reach of me and none of them look back!

I walk through grocery stores and find women away from their basket with their purse in the cart. Lastly, I drive around and observe a number of women jogging with iPods plugged into their ears...some even at night.

All of these acts are indicators to the predator, who observes you from a distance, that you are a good choice as his next victim. This is why it's critical that you heighten your awareness and eliminate all possible distractions while in public.

There's a saying in the martial arts world, "Wherever you are...be there." This simply means to be present in the moment and not daydreaming or being preoccupied with the past or the future.

If you focus on what is happening in the now and practice good safety habits as outlined in this chapter, your awareness skills will greatly improve.

Let's look at the different types of awareness:

- Criminal/predator Awareness
- Situational /present Awareness
- Self-awareness

Criminal awareness is accomplished by staying tuned in to what is going on in the area through all mediums, including: TV, radio, Internet and newspapers. Talk with your neighbors, co-workers and friends about recent crime in their area. Check the police blotter section in your local paper to learn about crimes that are happening all around you. Join or create a neighborhood watch program to help protect your community. Be proactive!

Situational awareness is being aware of what is happening at the present moment. Is this location safe? Are the suspicious looking teenagers hanging around the store or parking lot up to something? How many exit doors are in this establishment? Is someone following me? This is not fear; this is your survival instinct performing a quick assessment of the area so you don't find yourself walking into the lions' den.

You must stay off your cell phone and other listening devices while out in public. Predators look for women who are not paying attention to their surroundings. These devices impede one of your main senses...hearing! We don't have eyes in the back of our heads, so we rely heavily on our ability to hear someone walking up on us from behind.

Self-awareness involves taking a survey of yourself from a physical, mental and emotional standpoint. Many people don't realize that their physical appearance tells a story of their mental or emotional state. For example, when you're sick or sad, your outer appearance may include:

- Sad eyes
- Body drawn in and shoulders drooped
- Head hung
- Slow moving
- Withdrawn
- Low energy

On the other hand, a person who is happy or excited walks with purpose, smiles, has good posture and is filled with energy. This is why it is said that 55% of communication is through body language, 38% voice and vocal clues, and 7% words. Remember this the next time you're having a conversation and observe which speaks louder to you, their words or their body language.

Take a minute and do a quick self-assessment by asking yourself the following questions:

- Am I a confident person?
- Am I an aggressive person?
- Do I have a short temper?
- Am I confrontational?
- Am I overweight?
- Am I in good physical shape?
- Can I defend myself, or a loved one if attacked?
- Do I function well under stress?

This type of assessment could reveal the fact that you are unconsciously attracting trouble to yourself and allows you to take the necessary steps to correct it.

From this day forth, commit yourself to mastering the necessary awareness and avoidance skills that could help keep you and your loved ones safe and out of harms way.

Chapter 3: Fear Factor

Let's look at the definition of fear according to Webster's Dictionary. It means to "be afraid, feel anxious or apprehensive about a possible or probable situation or event; an emotion experienced in anticipation of some specific pain or danger (Usually accompanied by a desire to fight or flee)."

Note: the definition states the "anticipation" of pain or danger, not pain or danger itself. This is why we say that fear is nothing more than "False Evidence Appearing Real!" It is critical to your survival that you understand the difference between "perceived danger" and "real danger" so that you can take full advantage of your God-given survival instincts.

For example, imagine pulling up to the mall to finish some last minute shopping, and as you get out of the car you begin to say to yourself, "I'm all alone, what if someone's watching me? What if they attack me? What if they have a gun, take me to another location and rape me?" Then while in the store, you notice a man looking at you and you repeat the same self-defeating thoughts. When, in reality, he is just admiring your dress. This is what is called perceived danger, and for that moment your subconscious, which doesn't know the difference between what's real and what isn't, reads this signal of danger and immediately sends certain impulses to your nervous system and releases certain chemicals into your bloodstream to prepare you to either fight or run.

Now, don't get me wrong, the thought of becoming a victim of a violent crime is disturbing; however, unmanaged fear can not only retard your survival instincts, but also your health and overall quality of life.

Being safety conscious does not mean that you have to be fearful or paranoid about leaving your home. It simply means being aware of the times you're living in and taking the necessary steps to protect yourself and your loved ones.

A wise teacher once said to me, "If you accept, your response will always be right!" What he was saying, in terms of managing fear, was that if you recognize and accept the fact that you are living in violent times, then your natural, God-given instincts will guide you in the right direction. Your priorities will change, you will start taking the necessary precautions, including taking time to learn awareness and avoidance skills to help drastically reduce your chances of becoming a victim.

Turning fear into fury

So, how do we turn fear into fury? First, you need to understand what happens to you internally as well as physically when your survival instincts sense danger, then gain control of that particular response. Next, you must BELIEVE that you are a survivor and condition your mind and body, through awareness and physical training, in an environment that brings you as close to the reality of being attacked as possible. This is how you develop what we call killer instinct. Please, don't let anyone fool you, without the ability to switch on this survival instinct, you simply won't have the necessary confidence to protect yourself. Remember, a predator can smell fear a mile away!

Once your killer instinct is developed, a predator will take one look into your eyes and walk away because he will see the eyes of a survivor and not a victim.

Fight or flight response

Now look at what happens to you when your body is triggered by fear. Do you remember being frightened by someone or found yourself eye to eye with a vicious dog? What was your experience? Did you: jump or freeze, did your eyes widen, heart race, muscles tense up, vision become tunneled or did you have the urge to go to the bathroom? If so, then you experienced what is called an *adrenal dump*.

Flight Adrenaline, also known as *norepinephrine,* is a chemical that the body releases into the blood stream under the stress of what it perceived to be a dangerous situation. Notice I said "perceived" danger, because this chemical is often released when there isn't any real danger. For example, someone who has a fear of public speaking and is asked to stand up and address a crowd might experience butterflies, shallow breathing and even a rapid heartbeat. These false signals eventually handicap your true survival instincts, which can leave you susceptible to a surprise attack. However, if the danger is real, this flight response will prepare your body to react with abnormal strength and speed, getting you away from the threat as quickly as possible.

Fight adrenaline response, also known as *epinephrine,* diminishes your peripheral senses, giving you a laser-like focus on the threat itself. You become faster, stronger and your pain threshold increases from mild to superhuman. A classic example of this type of response is that of a mother, who in fear of losing her baby, lifted the back corner of a car off of her child. This mother's superhuman strength was the result of her fear of losing her child, and shows how your body's response to fear can actually save a life!

Here are 10 steps for turning fear into fury:

1. Develop a high level of awareness.

2. Be constantly aware of any potentially serious situations, i.e. a near accident or someone scaring you. Take notes of your response and strive to be in control.

3. Understand the difference between perceived danger and real danger.

4. Be aware and knowledgeable of the reality of the fight or flight response.

5. Learn reality self-defense skills.

6. See yourself in a situation and feel the response.

7. Develop your killer instinct thru scenario based training.

8. Cultivate the will to survive.

9. Be physically fit.

10. Believe in yourself and your skills.

Remember, fear is a gift if used for its intended purpose, which is to alert and prepare you for real danger. Commit yourself to mastering your fears on a daily basis, and the benefits you'll receive will be much more than just keen perception - you will awaken the survivor within!

Finding the right school

Now, with that said, don't run out and join the first Karate or Kung Fu school you see. Traditional arts are good for those who want to spend years learning traditional culture and ancient martial art techniques. However, for the person whose focus is on real world self-defense, you need to find an instructor who teaches a "reality-based" self-defense program. A huge part of this program should focus on awareness and avoidance skills and the rest on physical techniques.

The techniques should be very simple to perform and should not require brute strength. It should eventually progress to mock scenario training, meaning you're put in a situation where you're attacked while getting in or out of your vehicle, leaving a building or any other common attacks used by today's predators. This type of training is very empowering and has helped countless women overcome their fears.

Below is a list of questions to ask a school owner before joining his/her school:

- How long have you studied martial arts? What style?

- How long have you been teaching martial arts?

- Is your program "reality-based" self defense?

- Do you teach techniques that are women specific?

- What components make up your self-defense program? (The answer should include the following: physical fitness, awareness and avoidance training, adrenal stress response training (scenario training), de-escalation skill training, and reality based self-defense training.)

- Do you currently have women in your program?

- Do you teach awareness and avoidance skills? (If they say yes, ask them what in particular is taught.)

- Do you provide instruction on the use of personal safety devices? Which ones in particular?

- Do you have references or testimonials from women who have taken your course?

- Would you mind if I observe your program? Also, ask for a demo from one of the women in the class.

These questions will greatly assist you in finding the right school for your specific needs.

Fight or Flight Sources:
You: Staying Young, by Michael F. Roizen, MD & Mehmet C. Oz, MD
Mindtools.com
The Original Martial Arts Encyclopedia, John Corcoran, Emil Farkas & Stuart Sobel

Chapter 4: Home Safety

There was a time when our homes were considered a safe haven. We used to be able to leave the front door open, invite sales or service men in without checking their credentials and willingly offer assistance to a stranger in need.

Well those days are long gone. Within the last several years, there has been an explosion of violent break-ins called "home invasions." Unlike burglary, where the criminal watches your home over a certain period of time, studies your travel habits and burglarizes your home while you're away, a home invasion takes place while you are present. It is difficult to track accurate statistics because in many states home invasion is not a crime. Police reports show that in most cases the intent of the invader is to rob you; however, many cases of home invasion have been committed for the sole purpose of raping, kidnapping, or torturing the victim.

Although this crime is happening everywhere, there are two recent cases in particular that stand out in my head. The first was in Connecticut. In July of 2007, according to reports, two paroled criminals terrorized a family for hours in their home. They sexually assaulted the mother and her two daughters, and then strangled the mother, left the father severely beaten and set the house on fire.

The second case was in Miami, Florida. In November 2007, according to reports, a well-known football star was killed in his home after being awakened by a noise in his living room. When he got up to investigate, he was shot in his bedroom doorway. Reports show that four invaders were in his home at the time of the incident.

Now, imagine sitting at the dinner table with your family, or just enjoying a movie together, and the next thing you know, a group of assailants is kicking your front door down, brandishing shotguns. They bound and gag you and your family and begin stealing all of your belongings. Worst case scenario - they rape or kill everyone in the house.

This is real. It's happening throughout the country and the perpetrators are getting bolder by the day. Do a quick search on the internet for *home invasions*, then brace yourself for what your are about to read. In some cases they disguise themselves as repairmen as an alternative way of getting into your home. For example, they may say that they are with the gas company and they're checking for possible gas leaks. Another may pose as a delivery person pretending to have flowers or special delivery packages for you to sign. Or, a stranger may appear at your door with the story that his vehicle has broken down or he has some form of medical emergency and requests to use your phone.

Rule 1: Never open your door for strangers!

Anyone arriving at your home unannounced, stating that they're checking for gas leaks, cable or telephone problems, should be told through your door that you don't have a problem in your home and to leave your property immediately! It is important that you say this in a very authoritative voice. Also, most gas, cable or telephone problems are checked from the outside!

As far as delivery persons, if it's an unexpected delivery, simply ask them to leave the item on the steps. If they say you need to sign for it, ask for ID and call the company to confirm the delivery and the person's name delivering it.

Remember, most people become victims because they let their guard down. Taking a few simple steps can greatly reduce your chance of becoming a victim.

Listed below are steps necessary to help keep you and your family safe while at home:

- Make sure your front door has a peep hole.

- As mentioned earlier, be sure to ask for a photo ID. Call the company to verify that they are legitimate. If they cannot be verified, immediately contact the police.

- Keep hedges and bushes trimmed to eliminate hiding spots known as "ambush zones".

- Make sure your home is well lit. Invest in motion sensored flood flights.

- Use deadbolts on all exterior doors - particularly Schlage Locks. Most others can be "bumped" open with a simple modified key. For more info, conduct an Internet search on "bump key".

- Place "Home Security System" stickers on your doors and windows. Statistics show that this alone will greatly reduce the chances of your home being targeted.

- Secure all windows before turning in at night. (Note: If you have children, take them with you to teach them about home safety. Remember, they learn by watching what they do.)

- Never hide your keys outside of your home; you never know who is watching. If you lose a set, change the locks immediately.

- Keep your cell phone on and close to your bed at night; have 911 programmed into your phone.

- Close your bedroom doors at night to create barriers. (If you have small children, invest in one of the many monitoring systems.)

Arriving home late

- If you work late or happen to arrive home late, scan the area for suspicious vehicles. As you pull into the driveway, beep your horn before exiting the vehicle to attract your neighbor's attention. It's in our nature to look out the window to see what's going on. (Simply put, it's called being nosey.)

- Make sure that everything you need to take in the house is in the front seat or gather it before exiting your vehicle. You don't want to get caught with your back turned.

- If you live with someone, be sure to let them know your estimated time of arrival. (Have them observe you while you're exiting your vehicle.)

- If you live alone, let a friend know your estimated time of arrival, then call once you're in the house.

- Invest in a good "monitored" home alarm system with sensors for all windows and motion detectors for each floor.

Home Invasion Sources: Washington Post, CBS Evening News, Miami Herald, Fox News, Scientific Frontline World News

Protection against Burglary

Because burglary is often committed while a person is away, the likelihood of someone being injured is highly unlikely. Unless of course the burglar attempts to burglarize your home while you're asleep and you startle him. In this case, do not try to be a hero and fight for your flat screen TV or stereo; give them an out, then call the police. You can always replace material things but you can't replace your life! The hero that chases and seriously harms a burglar will find himself facing criminal charges. The courts don't recognize a fleeing burglar as a threat. Simply put, don't shoot a burglar unless your life or your children's lives are in imminent danger.

Below is a list of preventive measures that will help reduce your chances of becoming a victim of burglary:

- Be sure your home is well lit with motion lights.

- Use alarm decals on your windows. This alone has been known to deter burglary.

- Invest in a good alarm system with window sensors and motion detectors.

- Use timers for your lights if you are away for any extended period of time.

- Secure all windows, patio and garage doors every night.

- Do not leave spare keys outside of your home. If you lose your key, change the lock immediately.

- Do not leave notes on your door for friends saying you'll be returning at a certain time.

- If you live alone, be sure your answering machine says, "We're not available at the moment."

Steps to take while on vacation:

- Ask a neighbor or family member to watch the house while you're away. Remember to leave a number so that they can reach you.

- Stop all delivery of newspapers or arrange for someone to pick them up.

- Use timers on lights, TV and radios to turn on and off at certain times.

- Make sure blinds and shades are closed.

- Consider investing in a "Robo Dog". This device sounds like a real barking dog and is activated using microwave technology. (My favorite.)

Chapter 5: Vehicle Safety

Carjacking is defined as "completed or attempted robbery of a motor vehicle by a stranger to the victim". This crime differs from vehicle theft in that the driver is present and threatened, or actual force is used to take the vehicle. According to Justice Dept Statistics:

- Carjacking victimization rates are highest in urban areas, followed by suburban and rural areas.

- Ninety-three percent (93%) of carjackings occurred in cities or suburbs.

- A weapon was used 74% of the time, of which:
    - Firearms were used 45% of the time
    - Knives were used 11% of the time
    - Other weapons were used 18% of the time

Since most carjackings have the potential of becoming deadly, serious precaution needs to be taken when out, or while parked in your vehicle. We all know that the number one rule while driving is to "keep your eyes on the road"; however, for personal safety, the number one rule while sitting idly at a night or parked, is "Keep your eyes in your mirror."

Source of statistics: U.S. Department of Justice

Below is a safety checklist to help reduce your chances of becoming a victim of carjacking:

- Be aware of your surroundings.

- Utilize your side and rear view mirrors. Carjacker's prefer the element of surprise. (Most victims state that they never saw their attacker coming!)

- While at a traffic light or a stop sign, keep at least a car length between your vehicle and the one in front of you. This will give you an escape route, providing the traffic pattern allows for it.

- If you are bumped slightly in the rear by a car of young males, do not get out of the car; pull over to a busy area and contact the police. (This carjacking tactic is currently being reported.)

- In the city, always drive with your doors locked and windows up.

- Park in well-lit areas and try to park as close to the establishment as possible.

- When feasible, use valet or an "attended" parking garage.

- Do not leave valuables visible in your vehicle.

While outside your vehicle

- As you walk to your vehicle, be alert to suspicious persons sitting in parked cars.

- Don't be afraid to ask for a Security escort, especially if your instincts tell you that something isn't right.

- When approaching your vehicle, make sure your keys are in your hand.

- Look under, around, and inside your vehicle before getting in.

- Teach your children the system of getting in and out of the vehicle quickly while checking their surroundings.

- If you are confronted by an armed carjacker, don't resist, give up your keys! You can always get another vehicle. Contact the police immediately.

- Never willingly go with a kidnapper; use a distraction technique and run in a zigzag pattern while screaming for help. (Statistics show that most victims taken to a second location don't return alive!)

- If you are forced into the back of your vehicle, make sure your cell phone is on and 911 is programmed in your phone so you can contact the police. (Many phones have GPS tracking. Check with police; varies in different locales.)

Chapter 6: Shopping Safety

According to statistics, one theft takes place every 4 seconds in this country and a robbery take place every 49 seconds. What's even scarier is that a lot of these attacks are now happening in broad daylight.

Recently, in a suburban neighborhood in Maryland, a woman was robbed inside a grocery store by three young thugs who followed her into the store. They simply snatched her purse and ran out of the store - in broad daylight!

Mall areas in particular are also breeding grounds for attackers, especially during the months of August and December (back-to-school and Christmas season). The predators I've spoken with call this "peak season". They know you're going to be out in record numbers, carrying large sums of cash, and purchasing items that can easily be snatched and sold for a quick dollar. Again, they sift and sort, looking for potential victims who appear to be unaware of their surroundings, then wait for the opportune time to attack.

Below is a checklist to help keep you safe while shopping:

- Stay alert to your surroundings.

- Shop during daylight hours if possible. If you must shop at night, go with friends or family members. Remember, your chance of being attacked is greater after 8pm.

- Avoid wearing expensive jewelry.

- Dress comfortably.

- Avoid carrying large sums of cash.

- Pay for purchases with a check or credit card.

- If your credit cards are lost or stolen, notify the issuer immediately. (Program their number into your cell phone. This will greatly reduce your chances of being a victim of fraud.)

- Strap your purse on your shoulder and not across your neck. Also, be sure that your bag is pulled slightly to the front.

- If you feel someone is following you, switch to the opposite side of the mall, or enter a store and observe them from the window.

- Stay off your cell phone! It greatly impedes your ability to focus on your surroundings. If you have to use your cell phone, find a place to sit so you can observe while you talk.

- If you feel uncomfortable leaving the store or mall, notify Security and ask to be escorted to your vehicle.

By constantly being aware of your surroundings and following these simple tips, you will greatly reduce your chances of becoming a victim.

Statistical Source : FBI crime clock, 2004

Chapter 7: Rape Prevention

Rape has become the fastest growing crime against women in this country. Statistics show that a rape occurs every two minutes and sixty-eight percent are committed by someone the victim knows.

Here's the breakdown of rape victims:

- 11% are raped by intimate partners, i.e., husbands, boyfriends.

- 7% are raped by relatives.

- 50% are raped by friends or acquaintances.

What's worse is the fact that less than one-third of all rapes are reported to the authorities. The closer the relationship between the victim and the offender, the less likely the assault will be reported to the proper authorities. This makes it difficult to actually gauge the real statistical data on rape victims.

There is only one way to get these sexual predators off the street and that is to turn them in to the authorities. If not, these predators will continue to violate you and this vicious cycle of physical, mental, and emotional abuse will continue.

Before we go any further, let's look at what police and forensic psychologists call the four profiles of a rapist.

- The power-assertive rapist
- The anger-retaliation rapist
- The power-reassurance rapist
- The anger-excitation rapist

The *power-assertive rapist:* a self-centered, egotistical person with a macho image. He's more likely to find his victim in bars or other social gatherings. This person is physically and emotionally aggressive and will use force to control you. Although he may hit or threaten to kill you, that is not his intention. Generally, pleading with this type of rapist doesn't work. If you're going to resist, wait for the opportune time and explode with everything you have!

The *anger-retaliation rapist:* has resentment towards women. He typically doesn't want to kill, but has an explosive temper and wants to punish and brutalize his victims into submission. This individual looks for opportunity rather than any particular person. He'll grab you on the street from behind and drag you behind a building, or some other secluded area. Be careful with this type of rapist - any attempt to resist may cause him to beat you senseless. Do not challenge or anger this particular rapist. If you can escape or incapacitate him, go for it.

The *power-reassurance rapist:* lacks the self-confidence and interpersonal skills to develop a relationship with a woman. He pre-selects his victims by stalking or peeping through their window, then later sneaks in and accosts them. This person typically fantasizes about being the victim's lover and attempts to play out a romantic experience. He uses minimal force, generally does not use a weapon, and is the easiest to dissuade. Screaming, crying, pleading and praying out loud are excellent tools to use against this type of rapist. If this doesn't work...defend yourself!

The *anger-excitation rapist:* your sadistic rapist - the most cunning and dangerous of them all. His sexual satisfaction comes from inflicting pain on his victims. He will tie up, gag, and repeatedly rape his victims over a period of time; eventually he kills them. This person typically has total control over his victims - leaving no chance for escape. In this case, your best chance is to try and outsmart him by convincing him to untie you, and then plan your escape.

Note: two thirds of all rapes are committed by power rapists. Women who didn't have any self-defense skills were able to foil their attacker's rape attempt by screaming and fighting back.

Now that you know the different profiles of a rapist, you must rely heavily on your instincts as well as your awareness and avoidance skills to help keep yourself out of harms way. Be prepared!

Source:
Profiling Violent Crimes, R.M Holmes, S.T. Holmes
Psychology Today, Nov 1992

Basic terminology

Below is a partial list of crimes of a sexual nature. *No means No;* the court views these acts, committed against your will, as a crime!

Rape - forced sexual intercourse with a woman, including both psychological coercion and physical force. Forced intercourse means vaginal, anal or oral penetration by the offender. (This definition also includes penetration using foreign objects.)

Sexual Assault - completed or attempted attack generally involving unwanted sexual contact between the victim and offender. It may or may not involve force and includes acts such as grabbing or fondling. The mere verbal threat can constitute sexual assault.

Assault with intent to rape - a victim is violently attacked for the sole purpose of gratifying lust. A charge of this nature must show that the attack was sexually motivated and not an intent to rob the victim.

Note: Historically a man could not be found guilty of raping his wife. Today, most states make it a crime for a husband to force himself on his wife. *No means No!* (Check your local laws, as they may differ from state to state.)

Source: Everybody's Guide to the Law by Melvin Belli & Allen Wilkinson

More Rape/ Sexual Assault Statistics

- 25% of rapes take place in public areas or parking lots.

- 63% of rapes occur between 6pm and 6 am.

- Over 50% of rape victims were under the influence of alcohol or drugs.

- 47% of victims received physical injuries as a result of the assault.

- Last but not least, over 70% of assaults were committed without a weapon.

The last statistic shows why every woman should know basic self-defense skills.

Statistics Sources:
U.S. Dept of Justice (National Crime Survey, 2003)
FBI (Uniform Crime Stats, 1996)
US Justice Dept

Below is a list to help you avoid becoming a victim of rape. (Note: since most rapes occur by someone the victim knows, you must rely on good judgment as well as your natural instincts to help keep you out of harms way):

- While out at night be sure to travel with friends.

- Trust your instincts! If you feel uneasy about a

person that you are on a date with, discretely call someone and let them know. End the date and leave immediately.

- If you must travel alone at night, make sure someone knows where you are as well as your estimated time of return.

- Avoid parking on dark, unattended parking lots (use valet when feasible).

- If at a club or party, never leave your drink on the table or you could become a victim of date rape.

- Always carry a personal safety weapon like the personal alarm, Defender key chain, or mace. Please note: these items cannot be taken into a government or federal building.

- When leaving a mall alone at night, try to walk with a crowd or ask security to escort you to your vehicle.

- Take a self-defense/rape prevention course.

Resources:

Check the following websites for sex offenders in your neighborhood:
    www.intelius.com
    www.nationalalertregister.com
    www.familywatchdog.us

What to do if attacked

If you find yourself in immediate danger of being raped, here is a list of things you can do:

- Scream, "Rape, I don't know this man!" and run. Screaming the word "fire" is also an option.

- Stall, speak calmly and rationally; do not plead, cry or give any indication that you are scared.

- Urinate or vomit on yourself; tell him you have an infection - anything to deter him.

- Observe as much as you can about him - hair color, eyes, scars, tattoos, height and weight. This will make it easier for police to identify the predator.

- Fight back - statistics show that women who fight back are less likely to be raped. Use the adrenaline that's streaming through your veins and explode into him like a raging survivor!

If you are raped:

- Call the police immediately.

- Do not bathe, shower or douche. If you do change clothes, place them in a plastic bag and seal it.

- Confide in someone for counseling. Rape is a very traumatic experience. Contact the rape crisis center and arrange to speak to a counselor. Remember, only you can keep these predators off the streets. Whether it's an ex-husband, boyfriend, date or stranger...rape is rape!

Internet Dating Safety

In today's world, going on a date with a stranger can be a serious gamble. With the Internet quickly becoming the preferred way of meeting new people, the risk is even greater. More and more reports are being released about women falling victim to sexual predators online. Now with such social sites as MySpace and Craig's list, predators are finding it easier to lure women into their web.

Although on the surface this method of meeting someone appears safe, one of the major drawbacks is that you have no clue who you are chatting with. Technically, this also holds true for the person you meet face to face as well, but at least you can observe him and see if his words match his body language. The predator knows this, so he sets up a dummy email account and tells you what you want to hear. He may even meet with you a few times to get you to lower your guard a little. Before you realize what's happening, you're being violated.

The following is a true story:

A woman was brutally killed in Baltimore, Maryland by a man she met a few hours earlier on MySpace. While riding to his home, she told him that she changed her mind and didn't want to go. He allegedly became enraged and pulled over, threw her out of the car and beat her to death. Beware...this is happening all over the country to women of all ages, especially teenagers!

It is estimated that over 40 million people are using the Internet for dating and socializing each month. If you decide to use the Internet for dating, there are services you can use to increase your level of security.

Below is a list of internet dating safety services:

www.Webdate.com   Uses real-time video to interview possible candidates.

www.honestyonline.com   Provides background checks and other services.

www.safedate.com   Provides background checks and other services.

www.detectivetoday.net Provides free background checks and other services.

www.courtrecords.org   Provides criminal background checks.

If you use choose to use this method of dating, I highly recommend that you do the following:

- Ask the dating company what security measures are in place to properly screen the participants.

- Set up an email address strictly for this service.

- If you're going to post a photo, change the city on your profile.

- Take your time, don't be in a rush to give out your phone number or meet them for a date. Find out as much as you can about the person.

Prior to going on a date, use one of the services above to check his background. Your fact-finding mission should include not only his name, but what he does for a living and where he works and lives.

There is no need to pay someone to do this for you, just go to: www.zabasearch.com or www.courtrecords.org. Note: There is a nominal fee for Zaba search services. These services will verify his previous and current residence.

If you decide to meet this person:

- Tell a family member or trusted friend what you're doing or have someone join you.

- Meet at a busy place like a coffee shop or a bookstore.

- Have someone call you during the date to check on you. Reply by saying. "Yes, I'm still here. I'll call you if I'm going to be late." This way your date knows that not only does someone know where you are, they also know your departure time.

- At the conclusion of your meeting, while in his presence, pick up the phone and tell the person that you are leaving now.

Other Dating Tips

- Let your date know in advance what your expectations are concerning intimacy. Don't allow any touching.

- If possible, drive your vehicle to the agreed upon location. If you do allow him to pick you up, carry cash for cab fare.

- As stated earlier, contact a friend before, during, and after the date so someone is aware of your whereabouts.

- Make sure your body language doesn't send the wrong message. (Note: 55% of communication is via body language.)

- Trust your instincts - if something doesn't feel right, call your friend and leave.

- Practice self-defense.

- Carry a personal safety weapon like the Defender keychain, personal alarm, or mace.

Popular date rape drug

Rohypnol, also known as "roofies", is a sedative that's 10 times more powerful then valium. It is produced and sold legally by prescription in Europe and Latin America. Although it is illegal in the U.S., predators are buying it on the streets and the internet everyday. On the street it is called "forget pill", "trip and fall", and "mind eraser".

Rohypnol is a very small, tasteless and odorless drug that will dissolve relatively quickly in liquid. It normally takes effect in or around 10 minutes or so and leaves its victims very disoriented before they pass out. Most victims of this powerful drug report having very little or no recollection of what happened. The predator's method is, while out at a social gathering or club, to slip it in your drink or food while you're away from the table. Next, when you start to feel disoriented, they play it off as if you had too many drinks and offer to help you to your car. They then either take you home or to another location and rape you. When you wake up, you will hardly remember what happened. This usually makes it difficult for you to assist the police in finding your attacker.

Rule #1, never accept drinks from someone you don't know well or trust. If offered a drink from a date, walk to the bar with him and receive your drink from the bartender. Also, never leave your drink unattended, not even for a few seconds. If you're out with your friends and one of them appears to be a victim of this drug, keep them there with you and contact the police. Educate your family and friends about this drug. Remember, always travel with a friend at night and be aware and alert to your surroundings.

Source: womenshealth.gov

Chapter 8: Domestic Violence

Are you sleeping with the enemy?

Domestic violence is currently the leading cause of injury to women in America. They are more likely to be assaulted, raped, or killed by a male partner than by any other type of assailant. Accurate information on the extent of domestic violence is challenging to obtain because of serious under-reporting. However, it is estimated that one in four women in America will be assaulted by a domestic partner in her lifetime. Not only that, 20% to 30% of the women treated in emergency rooms were there as a result of physical abuse by their partners.

Whenever I speak on this subject at my personal safety seminars, it gets so quiet that you can hear a pin drop. As I look into the eyes of some of the participants, I see pain and undue suffering. Knowing that it's a touchy subject, I first try to connect with them by telling them that they deserve better and express the fact that any man who puts his hands on a woman is a man who does not honor or respect womanhood.

I also tell them about the countless cowards I've had to process into the prison system who had either badly beaten or killed their girlfriends/spouses. One abuser that I will never forget, beat his girlfriend, threw her in the trunk of her car, set her on fire and left her for dead.

Anatomy of an abuser

If you look closely enough, you can spot an abuser a mile away. Just observe the way he treats his mother, sister or other women he comes into contact with. Observe his treatment of the waitress while at a restaurant, or any other venue. If he shows any signs of aggressiveness, belittles, berates or insults her in any way, he is sending you a signal that he is a possible abuser. Other signs include:

- Low self-esteem
- Defensiveness
- High power/control needs
- Low stress tolerance
- Denial/justification of own violence
- Possessiveness/jealousy of partner
- Verbal aggressiveness
- Negative attitude towards women

In addition, most abusers have experienced violence in the family, abuse as a child, and or alcohol or drug abuse.

It is critical that you read the writing on the wall early in a relationship, before you get trapped and start justifying his controlling and violent actions. I submit to you, if you make it clear in the beginning that you do not allow anyone to yell at you or try to control you in anyway, he will have to choose to either face his fears or lose you!

Now, the key here is "YOU MUST MEAN WHAT YOU SAY AND SHOW IT IN YOUR ACTIONS!" If not, like the predator he is, he will sense weakness and play on it to cover his own fears and weaknesses.

Remember: "Rudeness is a weak man's imitation of strength". Be strong and know that you deserve better.

Statistical facts

You must do everything in your power to avoid becoming a victim of domestic violence. Remember, it's not only you who is affected, but your children, family and friends all lose in one way or another. Look at the statistics below and know that domestic violence is a serious problem in this country:

- Every nine seconds in the United States a woman is assaulted and beaten.

- Domestic violence is the number one cause of emergency room visits by women. 73% of the battered women that seek an emergency medical service have already separated from the abuser.

- Everyday four women are murdered by their boyfriends or husbands.

- The number one cause of women's injuries is abuse at home. This abuse happens more often than car accidents, muggings, and rapes combined.

- Battery often occurs during pregnancy. One study found that 37% of pregnant women, across all classes and education lines, were physically abused during pregnancy.

- When only spousal abuse was considered, divorced or separated men committed 79% of the assaults and husbands committed 21%.

- Abusive partners harassed 74% of the employed battered women at work, either in person or over the telephone, causing 20% to lose their jobs.

- More than 50% of child abductions resulted from domestic violence.

- More than half of battered women stay with their batterer because they do not feel they could support themselves and their children alone.

- Women are more likely to be killed when attempting to leave the abuser. In fact, they are at a 75% higher risk than those who stay.

- The chance of abuse and rape of children is 1500% higher in households where domestic violence occurs.

- 50% of the homeless women and children in the US are fleeing abuse.

Sources: National Domestic Violence Hotline website
National Violence Against Women Survey
(NCJRS) 2000
National Crime Victim Survey 2000
U.S. Departmentt of Justice (94/98)
National Center for Victims of Crime

Ask yourself the following questions and if you answer yes to any of these, you could be a victim of domestic abuse:

- Has your partner ever used profanity towards you or yelled at you in a threatening manner?

- Have you ever been physically hurt, i.e., pinched, pushed, punched or even kicked by your partner or ex-partner?

- Has your partner ever threatened to harm you to get you to do something?

- Are you ever afraid of your partner? Are you ever afraid of going home? Does he/she make you feel unsafe?

- Do you feel like you are being isolated from friends and family by your partner?

- Has your partner tried to keep you from doing things that are important to you?

- Have you ever been forced by your partner to have sex when you did not want to?

- Has your partner ever insisted on having unsafe sex against your will?

What to do if you are a victim of abuse

If you or someone you know is affected by domestic violence, please call the National Domestic Violence Helpline at 1-800-799-7233/1-800-799-SAFE. This is a confidential telephone number. Other contact numbers include:

- The National Coalition Against Domestic Violence: 1-303-839-1852.

- Battered Women's Justice Project: 1-800-903-0111.

- The Health Resource Center on Domestic Violence: 1-800-792-2873.

The following website: www.requestlegalhelp.com, offers legal assistance to battered women.

Please take advantage of these resources that are available to you so that we can help eliminate domestic violence.

Chapter 9: Voyeurism

What you don't know about voyeurism could land you on the Internet - naked!

With today's high tech video recording equipment now available to the general public, millions of women will find themselves victims of video voyeurism.

Simply put, video voyeurism is committed whenever someone, with indecent intent, takes a still picture or video of you in a private dwelling without your consent.

In 2004, President Bush signed into law the Video Voyeurism Prevention Act (Source: Global Legal Information Network, www.GlIN.gov) which makes it a crime to capture naked or undergarment covered images of a person where the person has an "expectation of privacy".

For example, a Long Island woman was spied on by her landlord for months after he hid a mini camera in a smoke detector on the ceiling above her bed. In another case, a woman was standing at an ice cream booth and a man secretly lowered his video camera so that he could film up her dress. Believe it or not, he is not guilty of a crime! Why, because the law does not apply to filming people in public places, even if it's underneath their clothes.

See for yourself how millions of women are being violated all over the world. Do an Internet search on "upskirting" and see what comes up. You or someone you know could be exposed to the entire world and not even know it. This violation of privacy is putting women at great risk of becoming a victim of sexual assault.

Some of the techniques voyeurs use in public places includes:

- Walking behind you, carrying a gym bag down by their ankles, with a hidden camera inside.

- Standing behind you with a mini-camera planted in their sneakers.

- Lowering their camera phone to view up your skirt while standing behind you.

- Placing their camera phone under the table where they're sitting and filming you.

- Appearing to be looking for a signal while catching you in a revealing position, i.e., getting out of the car, going up the stairs, bending over or reaching for something.

Steps to take to avoid being exposed in public:

- Be aware of your surroundings.

- Be conscious of who's behind you; don't allow anyone to stand too close to you.

- On escalators, turn sideways while holding onto the rails to observe those behind you.

- While sitting in a public place, i.e., a restaurant, be conscious of the positioning of your legs if you have a skirt or dress on.

Hiding places for cameras in private areas:

- Bathrooms or bedrooms

- Locker rooms or showers

- Hotel rooms

- Changing rooms in clothing stores

- Any other place where you could be observed while disrobed.

You must take extra precaution to avoid becoming a victim of this growing epidemic. Everyday, technology is advancing, making these cameras more inconspicuous than ever before. Look on the next page and see for yourself.

See if you can identify which of the items below are hidden cameras:

They all are!

Imagine your most intimate moment being secretly recorded and sold to an Internet voyeur who in turn exposes you to the entire world! Scary isn't it? This is the world of voyeurism and unless you've taken some serious measures to reduce your chances of becoming a victim of this rapidly growing epidemic, you could be next.

How these cameras work

Basically there are two types of cameras: wired and wireless.

The wired camera can be seen in most businesses, where the system is connected to a video recorder.

The wireless camera has a built in transmitter and can be easily hidden in something with no visible lens. It can be battery powered and actually beam the video through the air, sending a radio frequency (RF) signal to a receiver located a couple hundred feet to several miles away. This receiver then transmits the video to a TV, VCR, or other recording device. It could be at a neighbor's house, in a car down the street, or in a hotel room, and from there onto the internet!

To view some of the latest technology, visit: www.x10.com and click on cameras, then brace yourself for what you're about to see that's available to the general public. Some of these cameras are so small that they can hardly be detected without using counter-surveillance technology.

Please know that hidden cameras are designed to be difficult to detect. Some have components the size of a grape and a lens the size of a hole in the button of your shirt.

In order to uncover these types of cameras, you are going to need to invest in a hidden camera detector. These detectors pickup the RF signal in the room and alerts you by beeping or vibrating (highly recommended if you travel a lot). You simply turn it on and start scanning everything in the room, to include: radio, TV, smoke detectors, lights, books, mirrors etc.

They come in different sizes, starting as small as a lipstick holder up to the size of a cell phone. The price varies from fifty to a few hundred dollars depending on the quality. We are constantly evaluating the best products available, so contact us at 301-860-0030 before purchasing any security products.

What to do if you find a hidden camera?

- Stay calm! Do not alert the person that you know about the camera.

- Cover the lens by putting a towel over it or a piece of tape.

- If you're at a hotel and you find a camera, do not notify them. Keep in mind that it may or may not have been planted by an employee with the hotel's knowledge.

- Contact the police and pursue legal action.

Steps to take to protect your home from peeping toms:

- Purchase thick curtains.

- Keep curtains and blinds tightly shut, especially at night and in private areas of the house.

- Be mindful of who you let into your home - this includes your children's friends.

- Designate certain areas for visitors to be in your home.

- Install lights with a motion detector outside of the home.

- Purchase window alarms for vulnerable areas of the house, i.e., bathrooms, bedrooms, downstairs windows.

- Talk and share info with neighbors about unusual visitors or loitering in the neighborhood.

- Purchase a motion detector with a remote barking dog sound alert.

- Plant short bushes near the windows to make it difficult to stand or climb.

By taking these simple steps, you will greatly reduce your chances of becoming a victim of voyeurism.

Chapter 10: Personal Protection Devices

At my workshops, I often speak to women about having layers of protection in place to make it difficult for a predator to successfully attack them. One of the layers I highly recommend is carrying some type of personal safety device that will inflict enough pain to allow them to escape from harm.

The following devices are used all over the country as a means of personal protection. Please note: some of these items may be illegal to carry in your state. Check your local laws before investing in any of these items.

Defense spray

There are dozens of sprays on the market today, each one boasting to be better than the others. As a member of the Emergency Response Team at the Department of Corrections, we were required to go through a live test of the chemical agent Oleoresin Capsicum, also known as "OC" spray. The test went as follow:

We stood in front of a bucket of water while the instructor shot the spray directly in our faces. After a few seconds we were allowed to wash it off and this was my reaction to this highly effective agent. I instantly lost my breath, my eyes slammed shut and felt as if they were on fire; the more water I put on my face the more it seemed to burn. It took me at least twenty minutes to regain my composure, where I was able to breathe normally and actually see something. Needless to say, this experiment sold me on the effectiveness of this particular spray.

OC spray is not an irritant but an inflammatory agent which causes the eyes to slam shut, the capillaries to dilate and temporary blindness to occur. It also takes your breath away by instantly causing inflammation of the breathing tissues. If used properly, it will cause your attacker to stop in his tracks.

There are other sprays available such as *Chloraceteophenone* (CN) and *ortho-Chlorobenzalmalononitrile* (CS), which irritate the membrane tissues. They cause stinging pain, tearing and takes between 5 and 30 seconds to take effect. An attacker who is under the influence of drugs or alcohol and cannot feel any pain will be resistant to the effects of these agents. Also, an attacker with a knife will still have 5 to 30 seconds to attack you before it would take effect.

Tactical use of the spray

First, you must understand that a typical attack will more than likely be by surprise. Knowing this, you want to be sure that your spray is easily accessible. Most women have it in their purse which makes it difficult to use if they are suddenly accosted. You have a better chance of effectively using it if it is on your keychain with your thumb on the trigger in the ready position. I recommend the new "mace-ring" that is worn on your index finger. I teach my students that if approached, to step into their interview stance with their hands up and when the opportunity presents itself: make a fist and squeeze the irritant right in the assailant's face and run.

It is important that you constantly train with someone so if the time comes when you have to use it, you won't panic!

Practice different scenarios, for example, getting in and out of your car, entering your home, leaving the store, or being approached by a stranger. Remember to maintain a safe distance between you and the would-be attacker. Eight to ten feet should allow you ample time to use your defense spray if attacked.

Note: Be mindful of wind direction so you don't wind up with the chemical in your eyes.

Source: Prince George's Department of Corrections Training Academy

Stun guns

The stun gun, a popular defense weapon, is a small handheld device that delivers a tremendous amount of electrical charge into the nervous system. Although direct contact is required, this device can easily render a would-be assailant senseless in a matter of seconds. When you press the trigger, the sound alone is enough to scare an attacker away.

Some of the latest models come in all shapes and sizes and mimic typical handheld devices, i.e., cell phones and iPods. There are two small prongs that protrude on the front of the device. Once the trigger is pulled and contact is made to the attacker's body, a high voltage is sent into the nervous system, causing rapid muscle movement and a dazed mental state.

There are different power levels for stun guns, which range from 65.000 to 850.000 volts. A 100.000 volt stun gun will cause pain and disorientation but may not necessarily take him down. However, a 300.000 volt weapon will give you more takedown power, allowing you amble time to escape. These devices will also work through clothing up to two inches thick but you must maintain body contact as long as possible.

Depending on the voltage, a stun gun can:

- in one-half second, stun your attacker and cause muscle contractions.

- in one or two seconds, cause more intense muscle contractions as well as disorientation.

- in three or more seconds, drop your attacker, sending him into a state of dysfunction and temporary loss of motor skills for five to fifteen minutes.

Keep in mind that people will react differently to this weapon, so be prepared to hold it against your attacker's body as long as needed to incapacitate him and escape. Medical and scientific studies have shown that these personal safety devices are safe to use and do not have any negative effect on the heart.

Warning: If you do not learn to use this weapon in the proper manner, it will be useless and could possibly be used against you. There have been a number of incidents in which the attacker actually took the weapon from their victim and used it on them. If you are going to invest in one of these weapons, be sure to invest in the training that will give you the necessary skills needed to possibly foil an attack.

Some basic tips:

- Invest in a model that looks like a cell phone or some other state of the art product, as this will make it easier for you to utilize the element of surprise when confronted by an attacker.

- Before leaving your home, check the batteries to be sure they are fully charged.

- While walking at night, be sure to have it in your hand with your finger on the trigger button.

- Train with a partner, using different scenarios such as: entering your home, getting out of your car, entering and exiting an elevator, etc. Practice until you can instinctively respond without thinking about what action to take.

- Seek out a qualified instructor to train you in a reality-based setting. This type of training will give you the heart-pumping rush you will feel in a real life situation.

Before investing in one of these devices, check your local laws on stun gun possession. These laws vary from state to state, so if you are traveling, make sure it's legal in that particular state.

The Keychain Weapon

This personal safety device is my weapon of choice. It's a small, five inch lightweight piece of metal that attaches to your keys and is easily concealed. It can be used to strike your attacker with both ends or to simply release a grab or chokehold.

This is exactly what happened to one of my seminar participants, who to this day, swears by her keychain:

One cold winter night, while in a grocery store parking lot, an attacker crept up and grabbed her from behind. She instinctively swung her keychain weapon, hitting him in the face, dropping him to his knees. The store manager ran out and held the man down until the police arrived. She later found out that the attacker's vehicle was running, which means he may have intended to abduct her.

Now, I'm not saying that the other weapons are not a good choice. But I've read far too many incidents where a woman sprayed herself in the face with mace or the attacker took the stun gun and used it on his victim. Not to mention the fact that a lot of times women place these items in their purse where it might be difficult to get to in the heat of the moment. With the Defender, it's right on your keychain and since your keys are <u>supposed</u> to be in your hands while you're walking to your vehicle or to your front door, you're less likely to be caught without it.

Note: Do not take this item to the airport or any Government facilities as it will be confiscated. Also, check your local laws to insure this personal safety weapon is legal in your state.

There is a section on how to effectively use this weapon in the last chapter of this book. If you would like more info on this item, visit www.safetykeychain.com.

Pepper Spray

Stun Gun

The "Defender"

Chapter 11: Self-Defense Attributes

"The ingredients that make it all work"

Before we get to the "how to" defend yourself portion of this book, it is imperative that we take a minute to understand some fundamental basics that are absolutely necessary for you to learn.

Earlier we discussed turning fear into fury to gain the psychological edge that's needed to effectively defend yourself. Now let's look at the physical attributes that will allow you to execute your counterattack to the point where you will be felt and not seen. Without the knowledge of how and when to make it work, all the martial arts training in the world won't help you in a real life situation. Let's look at the first attribute:

Speed

Speed plays a very important part in the delivery of your strike. Most predators look upon women as a weaker species and in most cases will invade their personal space. This mindset can work in your favor because he actually puts himself in range for a well-timed stunning technique. If executed correctly, the predator will have little time to react because he would have compromised his own reactionary gap (the distance between you and the predator). Do not draw your hand back to generate power or change your facial expression before your initial move; this will alert him that something is about to happen and will put him on the defensive.

How do we train for speed?

There are a number of ways you can train to drastically increase your speed. One simple method is to stand in front of a mirror, fold one arm over the other, relax your shoulders and arms, and without any excessive movement, snap your hand out towards the mirror, at face level, and back as fast as you can. Repeat this exercise for three sets of five repetitions. Now, the key is to focus on pulling the hand back from the mirror, not pushing it out. Think of snapping a towel out…the power is in the pull, not the push. This causes the towel to pop, which is also the point of impact. Remember to relax your muscles before releasing and to exhale sharply or yell on execution.

Another drill is to have a partner put one hand up, chest level, and stand back about one arm's length. Place your right hand on your chin as if you were contemplating something and place your left hand around your waist. Your objective is to hit your partner's hand before they move it. Remember, you must relax, stare at their chest and explode towards your partner's hand with the thought of pulling it back as fast as possible. I teach my students to imagine the target being hot coal and to try to hit their partner's hand five out of five times without getting burnt.

Over time, these simple exercises will give you cat-like reflexes where you will be felt and not seen.

Timing

The second attribute is timing. Having cat-like speed means nothing if you strike at the wrong time. For example, trying to execute a finger jab at your assailant's eyes while he is wielding a knife back and forth in front of your face would not be practical. However, waiting for him to lower the blade, away from your line of attack, would give you a better chance of jabbing his eyes without getting cut in the process. While we're here, I should also mention that timing and accuracy go hand in hand. Having perfect timing is also useless if you miss the target altogether. However, a fast, accurate and well-timed elbow strike on an attacker's jaw could render him unconscious.

How do we train for timing and accuracy?

There are many ways to develop these attributes; however one of the simplest ways is to have someone stand in front of you and then step towards you. When they move, step in as fast as you can and touch them on the shoulder before they can put their foot down. Next, do the same thing with their legs by launching a side-kick to their knee. Do not step up to kick, just raise your knee and deliver a fast side-kick.

This is what we call "stop-hit" - shutting down your assailant's intent by attacking a primary target and following through until he is down. Another simple training method is to practice countering your assailant's attack by using what we call "simultaneous parry (redirect) and strike". Have someone punch at you slowly and you parry the punch and counterstrike at the same time. Do this ten times. Repetition will help develop what we call "muscle memory" and allow you to execute without thought. In a real life situation, if you have to think about what to do, it's too late.

Power

It is critical that you understand and believe that you don't have to be a "Ms. Olympia" in order to develop striking power. We have a saying in Tai Chi, a form of moving meditation, that "your force is rooted in the legs, guided by the waist, and expressed through the arms".

In other words, your punch, palm strike, or elbow strike starts by twisting your rear leg. This twist starts the process of generating a tremendous amount of force which transfers through the waist, shoulders, and finally into the arms.

The formula for power is: weight x speed = power. For example, a person weighing 120 pounds will have to hit twice as fast as someone 220 pounds and over in order to generate the same amount of power. Now do you see how these attributes work hand in hand?

Another key component in generating power is balance. Without proper balance/alignment, you will lose most of your striking power before it even reaches your waist.

Try this: have someone hold a pad for you and try to strike it full power while on your tiptoes. Stand with your left foot forward in a fighting stance and throw a right horizontal elbow as hard as you can. Next, put your feet flat on the floor, bend your knees a little and throw the strike from this position. You should notice a tremendous difference in the amount of force you generate from a well-balanced stance. In real life this could be the difference between you just hitting your assailant and actually knocking him down.

If you practice these simple drills consistently, you will develop the skill and confidence that is needed to make the techniques in this book work.

Chapter 12: Fit to Survive

There are many self-defense books that teach a number of physical techniques for dealing with predators. However, very few talk about being in what I call "fighting shape". Now, you don't have to have the fitness level of a boxer, but you should be in good physical shape in the event you have to physically defend yourself or run.

I realize that this is a bold statement, but that's a reality most people don't want to hear. So as a result, volumes are being produced on women's self-defense without any mention of being "fit for battle". This attitude gives women a false sense of security and makes them even more susceptible to an attack. Not to mention that their confidence level will be extremely low, knowing that they are physically out of shape and therefore not able to put up a fight.

This is why we said in the awareness section that when you do your self-analysis, be honest with yourself and address all of your challenges accordingly. Notice that I said challenges and not weaknesses. Weakness is an attitude. If you believe that life's challenges are weaknesses, then you accept it as a reality and begin to either hide or justify its existence. Remember, the predator, when he sizes you up during the interview, reads you like a book, checking your physical stature, demeanor and confidence level...all in a matter of seconds.

Now, imagine that you are leaving a concert, walking to your car that is parked in the lot a block or so down the street and out of nowhere you are accosted by a knife-wielding rapist. You break away and the rapist starts to chase you.

About a block later, you are exhausted and totally out of breath. There you are on the ground, gasping for air, and he's standing over you getting ready to violate you. Now your chance of being raped is even greater because you have no fight left in you.

Don't be caught out of shape! Getting fit has many benefits besides being able to defend yourself, to include: toner muscles, a stronger heart, improved cardio, weight control, and of course fewer visits to the doctor. This all translates to a better quality of life.

Don't wait! Start developing your work-out regimen today. Join a gym, or better yet, join a martial arts school that teaches "reality based self-defense". This type of school will train you through "scenario conditioning" and will have you "fighting fit" in a relatively short period of time.

Simple fitness routine

There are countless ways to get in shape. Below is a simple workout you can do anywhere, on your own, for a minimum of twenty minutes a day, three times a week.

- Jumping rope: Five to ten minutes a day will improve your cardio level, coordination, and footwork.

- Shadow boxing: Put on a set of handwraps, turn on your favorite music and start punching in the mirror, on your toes, for three one-minute rounds with a thirty second rest. This is excellent for cardio conditioning, developing speed, focus, and agility.

- Crunches: Lie on your back, lift and cross your legs. Cross your arms over your chest and bring only your shoulders off the floor. Start out easy and work your way up to a hundred. (Strengthens your center.)

- Push-ups: Modified push-ups (on knees) are OK to start with. Eventually work your way up to 15-20 military pushups. (Works your chest, back of arms, and shoulders.)

- Triceps press: Find a chair, place your hands on the edge of the chair behind you, and extend your legs out in front of you, toes pointed up. Lower your body to the floor as far as you can then push up. Start out easy with five to ten repetitions and work your way up to twenty. (Works the back of the arms.)

- Squats: Fold your arms in front of you, step over with your right foot, shoulder-width apart and squat down until your thighs are parallel to the floor. Start out with as man has you can and work your way up to twenty-five or thirty. (Strengthens your thigh muscles.)

- Knee raises: Stand with your feet together, raise your hands over your head and interlock your fingers. Raise your knee as you lower your arms, alternating sides. Repeat 10 times. (Strengthens your lower abs.

Consider investing in a portable heavy-bag. You can normally find one of these in any sporting goods shop priced between $79 and $90. This is what we call the boxer's greatest secret. A few rounds on a heavy-bag and you'll be a fit, fat-burning, fighting machine.

Modified Push-ups

Keep your back and head straight. Be sure to inhale as you go down.

Go down as far as you can, then push up. Exhale while pushing up.

Triceps press

Extend your legs out and keep your arms straight. Inhale while lowering your weight.

Lower your body as far as you can and then push up. Exhale while pushing up.

Squats

Stand with feet shoulder width apart and arms folded in front of your chest. Inhale as you lower your body weight.

Squat down until your thighs are parallel to the floor and then come up. Exhale while pushing up.

Knee Raises

Stand with your feet together, raise your hands over your head, and interlock your fingers.

Raise your knee as you lower your arms, alternating sides.

Chapter 13: Fighting Back

"When your life is on the line"

This section covers everything from how to deal with a simple nuisance to a vicious rapist whose intent is to violate and or kill you.

The following is covered in this section:

- Vital targets

- Kicks

- Strikes

- Stances

- How to avoid a strike

- How to fall properly

- Quick releases from wrist/arm grabs

- Chokehold escapes

- Defense from the ground

- Rape defense

- How to use everyday items as a weapon

- The keychain weapon

VITAL TARGETS

"Hit him where it hurts"

Vital targets are vulnerable areas of the body that could stun or totally incapacitate your attacker. Be mindful of the fact that some areas require more force than others in order to be effective. In each caption, you will see the necessary force needed to affect that particular target.

PRIMARY TARGETS

Primary targets are areas on the body that have the potential to incapacitate your attacker with one well-focused strike. There are three primary targets that we use in our Personal Safety Program:

- Eyes

- Knee

- Groin

Finger strike to eyes, with fingers spread apart.

[Minimum force]

Front kick to groin.

[Medium force]

Side kick to knee.

[Maximum force]

SECONDARY TARGETS

Secondary targets are follow-up targets that can be struck after your initial strike to one of the 3 primary targets.

Keep in mind that, depending on the situation, a secondary target could very well incapacitate your attacker – giving you enough time to escape.

Some secondary targets include:

- Nose: palm-heel strike

- Ears: A solid palm smack

- Throat: A strong elbow strike

- Ribs: A sharp elbow strike

- Toes: A good heel stomp

As mentioned earlier, to be effective, all of these strikes require the necessary attributes, to include: speed, timing, power, the element of surprise and the proper mindset.

Palm strike to nose.

[Maximum force]

Slap the ears with your palms.

[Medium force]

Knuckle strike to throat.

[Medium force]

Elbow strike to ribs.

[Maximum force]

Front kick to shin.

[Maximum force]

Stomp to toes.

[Maximum force]

KICKS

There are 3 kicks that we teach in our program: side kick, front kick and round kick. As a rule, our kicks are thrown no higher than the waist. This reduces your chance of slipping or having your leg caught by your assailant.

FRONT KICK

From the fighting stance:

Raise your knee up.

Extend your foot out in front.

SIDE KICK

From the fighting stance:

Raise knee to waist level. Turn your hip over and pivot on supporting foot.

Extend your kick out knee level. Make sure your supporting leg is bent.

YOUR ARSENAL OF WEAPONS

Besides your mind, the two most powerful weapons you have are your elbows and knees. However, there are targets that do not have to be struck with maximum force to incapacitate your assailant. There are 7 simple weapons we teach in our program (keep in mind that there are more at your disposal, but theses are the ones we've selected):

The 7 weapons include:

- Elbows: Upward, side and downward strikes

- Knees: Upward and inward strikes

- Top of head: Head butt

- Fingers: Jabbing and raking

- Feet: Kicking vital targets

- Forearm: Neck strike

- Shin: Thigh strike

Elbow strikes:
- Horizontal
- Vertical
- Oblique

Knee strikes:
- Upward
- Inward

Head butt:
- Frontal
- Rear

Finger strike to eyes:
- Poke
- Rake

Heel to groin.

Forearm strike to neck.

Shin strike to thigh.

ELBOW STRIKES

VERTICAL

From the Interview
Stance:

Twist your waist and
throw an upward elbow
strike.

Twist and repeat on left
side.

ELBOW STRIKES

HORIZONTAL

From the Interview stance:

Twist your waist and throw a side elbow strike, with your right elbow. Be sure the left hand is protecting your ribs.

Twist and repeat on other side. Be sure to raise the heel of your back foot for maximum power.

STANCES

There are 2 types of stances we teach:

- Interview stance
- Fighting stance

INTERVIEW STANCE

Correct way:

<u>Option 1</u>

- Step back and raise both hands shoulder level. Knees slightly bent.

<u>Option 2</u>

- Step back with one foot and raise your front hand.

<u>Option 3</u>

- This time, raise both hands with finger tips touching and pointing forward.

Explanation:

One foot behind the
other, with your body
angled to the side,
gives you a firm root
and makes it difficult
to be pushed down.

INTERVIEW STANCE

Wrong way:

- Standing with your feet parallel, facing your assailant.

- You have no balance and can be easily knocked down.

FIGHTING STANCE

Right way:

Your body is turned to the side, back heel is raised, knees are bent, hands are up with your elbows by your side.

Wrong way:

Hands down, exposing your face. Your rear foot is directly behind front foot. This compromises your balance.

AVOIDING AN ATTACK
HOW TO AVOID A STRIKE

Moving off the line of a strike by stepping forward at a 45° degree angle, either left or right, protecting your face and body.

As the attacker punches with his left hand, step up and over to the right while parrying his strike and protecting your body. This keeps you in range to counter his strike.

Same as the other avoidance technique, step up and over to the left, parrying his right punch and protecting your body.

HOW TO BREAK YOUR FALL
FALLING FORWARD

From a standing position:

Bend your knees, tuck your chin and place your arms in front of you.

Kick your feet out from under you, bracing your fall with your forearm, turning your head either left or right to prevent hitting your head.

HOW TO BREAK YOUR FALL
FALLING BACKWARD

As the attacker catches
you off guard, place
your arms across your
chest, bend your knees
and tuck your chin.

Kick out one of your
legs, while keeping
your chin tucked
toward chest to avoid
hitting your head.

Allow your body to
naturally fall backwards as
your legs rise upward. Use
your hands to slap the
ground at a 45° angle to
minimize the impact of
hitting the ground.

DEFENSE AGAINST A NUISANCE

The nuisance puts his finger
in your face…

Using the opposite hand, grab
his finger with your first two
fingers and place your thumb
against his finger.

Flex your wrist down, bending
his index finger toward his
chest, forcing him to drop to the
ground. Note: Keep your
elbows close to your side.

Close-up of finger grab.

WRIST GRAB DEFENSE
QUICK RELEASES

Attacker grabs your
right wrist with his left
hand.

Immediately pull your
hand upward (while
stepping back).

WRIST GRAB DEFENSE
QUICK RELEASES (CONTINUED)

Variation:
Attacker grabs your
right wrist with his left
hand.

Instead of pulling up,
step back and turn your
hand to the side and pull
it out.

WRIST GRAB DEFENSE
QUICK RELEASES (CONTINUED)

Attacker grabs your
right wrist, using his
right hand.

Making a semi-circle
movement, point your
finger to the outside and
pullout.

Close-up of opposite
side wrist grab.

WRIST GRAB DEFENSE
DEFENSE AGAINST A GRAB

As the assailant approaches you, step back and assume your interview stance.

As he grabs your left wrist with his right hand...

Twist your back foot and throw a side elbow with your right arm to his jaw. Be sure to turn your waist for maximum power.

WRIST GRAB DEFENSE
CROSS GRAB

Attacker grabs your left wrist with his left arm.

Place your right hand on top of his hand to secure it. Circle your hand, counter-clockwise, and place your left hand on top of his forearm (as close to the wrist as possible and flex your wrist down toward his navel.)

SHOULDER GRAB DEFENSE
FRONT

As assailant approaches, step back in your interview stance.

When attacker grabs your right shoulder with his left arm, place your left hand on top of his hand to secure it. Circle your right arm up and over his wrist.

Turn your body inward toward his center. While still holding on to his hand, lower your elbow on his wrist and take him down.

SHOULDER GRAB DEFENSE
REAR

Attacker grabs your right shoulder with his right hand, turn to look and see which hand is on your shoulder.

Grab his hand with your left hand to secure it and raise your arm up and over his wrist.

While holding onto his hand, turn your body and drop your elbow over his forearm close to his wrist.

HAIR PULL DEFENSE
FRONT

Attacker grabs your hair from the front with his right hand.

Place both of your hands on his hand to secure it.

Now, lower your body and push your head forward and down, causing pressure at the attacker's wrist. Hold and press until he goes down.

HAIR PULL DEFENSE
REAR

Attacker grabs your hair
from the rear with his
right hand,

Grab and secure his
hand and circle to your
right (down and up in
clockwise motion).

As you turn toward
attacker, you cause his
wrist to twist, which
causes serious pain.

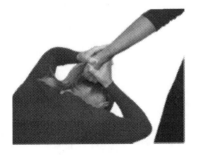

DEFENSE AGAINST A PUSH

Attacker attempts to push you down to the ground.

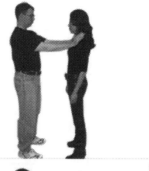

Quickly step back with your left leg and turn your body away from the push.

As he pushes through, turn toward him and strike him in the groin with your left knee.

DEFENSE AGAINST A PULL

As the attacker approaches you, step back with your right foot.

As he grabs and pulls you toward him, grab his hands and step forward with your left foot.

Drive your right knee into his groin and escape.

DEFENSE AGAINST A GRAB AND PUNCH

Attacker surprises you with a collar grab with his left hand.

Immediately grab his hand and zone (step) to the right and apply a finger jab to his eyes.

Turn and lower your body while dropping your forearm down into the crease of his elbow. This will take him down quickly.

Be sure to escape as quickly as possible!

BACKHAND SLAP DEFENSE

As attacker throws a backhand slap with his right hand, step up and over to your left and grab his arm with both hands.

While bracing his arm, throw a powerful shin kick to the side of his thigh area and run.

Option:

An alternative would be to throw a knee to his mid-thigh. Be sure to thrust your hips forward for maximum power.

CHOKE DEFENSE - FRONT

Attacker surprises you with a front choke.

Hold your breath and place your thumbs under his wrist and push up as you step back to release the hold.

While still holding onto his wrist, deliver a swift front kick to his groin and run!

CHOKE DEFENSE – REAR

Attacker surprises you from the rear and chokes you with his right arm. Hold your breath and immediately use both hands to pull his arm downward as you raise your heel up into his groin.

Trace your foot down the back of his leg and lock your foot behind his, then press your shin against his shin to take him down.

Once he falls, drop your knee on his ankle. Then escape!

BEAR HUG DEFENSE
ARMS OUT

As assailant grabs you, grab his hands and abruptly drop your weight to keep him from picking you up.

Quickly turn and execute a right elbow strike to his jaw.

Rotate quickly and elbow strike him on the left side.

While he's stunned, reach down and grab his leg just above the ankle and…

Abruptly pull his leg forward and upward.

Hold onto his leg until he falls, then escape!

BEAR-HUG DEFENSE
ARMS PINNED

As he grabs you, grab his
hands and immediately
drop your body weight.

Twist your hips outward,
to the right and step
behind your attacker.

Next, slam your left hand
into his groin, and run!

RAPE DEFENSE
FIGHTING FROM THE GROUND

Ground fighting position:

Turn to the side and raise your feet off the ground to defend yourself. Place your elbow by your face for protection.

As attacker approaches, shoot a side kick to his knee.

If he happens to get close to you, turn and lean back on both elbows, then front kick him in his groin using your heel.

LEG DRAG DEFENSE

As he grabs your right leg, hook his foot with your left leg.

This will keep him from moving while you reach up and grab his leg.

While pinching his leg with your left hand, strike inside his knee with your right fist and drop him to the floor.

Follow up with a heel strike to the groin. Quickly get up and run!

GROUND DEFENSE
FROM A PUSH

Attacker surprises you
and pushes you to the
ground.

Apply the "break-fall"
technique by first crossing
your hands in front of you.
Next, step back and bend
your knees.

Tuck your chin and break
your fall by smacking both
hands down to your sides.

GROUND DEFENSE (CONTINUED)

Immediately turn to your
right side, prop up on
your forearm with your
other arm shielding your
face. Draw your legs
closely to your body to
prepare to launch a side
kick.

Kick attacker's knee with
your left leg to stop him,
then quickly place the
same foot behind his foot.

Hook the back of his foot
tightly.

125

GROUND DEFENSE (CONTINUED)

Rise up and press your
shin forward against his
shin to take him down.

As he falls…

place both hands on the
ground and strike the
attacker in the groin
with a left side kick,
then run!

RAPE DEFENSE
HOW TO AVOID BEING HIT

This is considered an "open guard" position in which you close your knees together and raise your hips off the floor to prevent the attacker from hitting you.

This defensive move is from a "closed guard" position in which your legs are around his waist area. As he goes to strike, grab his hand and stop his punch by placing your feet at the bend of his elbow.

RAPE DEFENSE
AVOID BEING HIT (CONTINUED)

As he punches at you with his left hand, parry his punch to the side with your right hand.

Parry his right punch with your left hand.

Variation:
Cross your arms and parry his punch using your elbows.

RAPE DEFENSE
STRIKING OPTIONS

Elbow strike to the jaw or chin area.

A finger rake across the eyes.

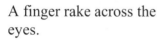

Grab the attacker's arm and abruptly strike him with a side elbow to his temple or jaw.

GETTING HIM OFF YOU
TURNING THE TABLES

While on your back,
shield your face with
both hands and place
your feet flat on the floor.

As he drives back to
strike you, quickly place
your arms on the ground
as you raise your hips and
slightly bump him
forward.

As he falls forward, grab
his right arm at the
elbow fold...

Pull his arm in and place your left foot on the outside of his foot.

Raise your hips up and begin to roll to your left.

After you have rolled him over to his back, immediately execute a strong punch to his groin and escape.

GETTING HIM OFF YOU
(OPTION 2)

This is a closed guard position in which you lock your legs around his waist while shielding your face.

As he attempts to strike, parry his punch with your right hand and rake his eyes with your left fingers.

Grab his right arm at the elbow with your left hand and elbow him in the jaw.

GUARD POSITION (CONTINUED)

Next, grab his head and drop your feet, turn sideways and scoot your hips out to your right. Place your right shin across his stomach and lay your left leg flat on the floor.

Pull on his arm, while at the same time sweeping his legs by pushing with your right leg and cutting back with your left leg.

Strike his groin with your right knee, elbow strike his jaw and escape.

BLOOD CHOKE DEFENSE (SLEEPER)

While on your back, shield your face with both hands and place your feet flat on the ground.

As he punches, parry his punch with your left hand and place your forearm on his neck.

Quickly reach up with your left hand, grasp your right hand, and squeeze. Ensure your hands are clasped tightly together – do not interlock your fingers.

WARNING: This technique could knock your attacker out!

RAPE DEFENSE
LEG CHOKE

While in the closed guard position, shield your face with both hands and lock your legs around attacker's waist.

As he punches, parry and grab his arm with both hands and pull it to the right side of your head.

Wrap your right leg around his neck and secure it with your left leg. Pull down with your left leg to choke him.

WARNING: This technique could knock your attacker out!

MAKESHIFT WEAPONS
HOW TO USE EVERYDAY ITEMS AS A WEAPON

This includes:

- Rolled up newspaper/magazine
- Hardcover book
- Purse strap

DEFENDING AGAINST A PUNCH
NEWSPAPER

As attacker punches with his right hand, step to the left on a 45 angle and deflect the punch on the outside of his arm.

As attacker punches with a left hand, step to the right at a 45 degree angle and deflect the punch on the outside of his arm.

You may also grab his arm and pull him toward you as you hit him with a backhand strike to the eyes.

DEFENDING AGAINST A PUNCH
NEWSPAPER (OPTION 2)

As attacker approaches you, step back.

As he punches, step to the right and parry his punch with your right hand. Next, execute a backhand strike to his face with the rolled up newspaper.

Circle his arm with your left arm and abruptly drop to your right knee, strike up into his groin with your forearm and escape.

DEFENSE AGAINST A CHOKE
NEWSPAPER (OPTION 3)

As the attacker approaches, step
back with your right foot.

As he reaches to choke you,
raise his arms upward with the
newspaper or magazine.

Now, quickly step forward with
your left foot (outside of his
right arm) jab him in the eye
with the newspaper and run.

DEFENSE AGAINST A CHOKE
BOOK

As the attacker approaches, ensure one foot is back and your hand is up.

As he surprises you with a frontal choke, hold your breath.

Push his arms upward with the book to release his hold.

Then step forward with your left foot and shove the book into his throat and escape.

PURSE STRAP

As the attacker approaches, ensure one foot is back and grasp your purse straps tightly together.

As he reaches out to grab you, step inside of his arm and finger jab him in the eyes.

Follow up with a head-butt to his nose.

Then reach over his head and wrap the strap around his neck and pull tightly.

PURSE STRAP (CONTINUED)

Drop to your left knee and pull him down to the floor.

As you pull him down, adjust your position by moving your right foot over so he doesn't fall on your leg, keeping him close to you.

Secure the choke with the purse straps, then escape.

KEYCHAIN WEAPON
The Defender

In this final section, you will learn:

- Proper stances
- 3 striking patterns
- Vital targets
- Defense against wrist grabs
- Choke escapes
- Bear-hug escapes

STANCES

With the Defender in your right hand, step back with your right foot and cross your arms, left over right.

Option 2: With the Defender still hidden, place one had up to create a barrier.

Fighting stance: Bend your knees and raise your back hand up to about chin level. Raise your back heel for mobility.

STRIKE PATTERN – SIDE TO SIDE

From the fighting stance:

Swing the Defender in a
horizontal movement,
across your body…

From right to left and return to
fighting stance.

UPWARD STRIKE

From the fighting stance:

Strike up and down in a vertical
movement.

THRUST STRIKE

As if pulling your keys
from your purse, prepare
to thrust forward in a
straight line.

Extend out as far as possible
with out locking your
elbows.

VITAL TARGETS

Vertical upward strike to the chin.

Horizontal strike across temple.

Vertical upward strike into groin.

Thrust strike into throat.

Hammer strike into back of hand.

QUICK RELEASES

Attacker grabs your left wrist with his right hand.

Turn your palm upward and place the Defender on his wrist.

Press downward on his wrist as you pull your hand up, releasing his grip.

VARIATION

Attacker grabs your left
wrist with his left hand.

Place the Defender
under his wrist bone and
your thumb on top of his
wrist.

Squeeze his wrist bone
with the Defender and
lift upward, releasing his
grip.

GRAB AND PUNCH DEFENSE

As the attacker grabs your shoulder with his right hand, grab his hand with your left hand and step up and over to your left.

At the same time execute a straight thrust into his throat area.

Next, drop your body weight and slam the Defender down into his elbow crease, forcing him to fall. Turn and escape.

FRONT CHOKE DEFENSE

As the attacker attempts to choke you, hold your breath, grab his right wrist with your left hand.

Place the Defender in the area under his bottom lip and press inward and down.

Press the Defender until he releases his hold. Follow up with another strike, and then run!

BEAR HUG DEFENSE

As the attacker grabs you from behind, grab his hands, step over to your right and immediately drop your body weight.

Hammer strike the back of his hand to release his grip.

Turn and look, strike him in the eye with Defender, and then run!

BEAR HUG DEFENSE (VARIATION)
ARMS OUT

As he grabs you around your waist, step over with your right foot and drop your body weight. Strike the back of his hand with a hammer strike.

As soon as he releases his hold, turn and throw a right elbow strike to his face.

Finish with a left elbow strike to the other side of his face, then escape.

KNIFE ATTACK DEFENSE

Attacker hides the
knife behind his back.

Attacker grabs you by the shirt
and puts a knife to your neck.

With the Defender in your left
hand, slide up between his arms
and place the Defender across
his wrist with your thumb on
top. Push the blade away from
your neck.

AGAINST A KNIFE ATTACK (CONTINUED)

Grab the other end with your right hand and squeeze his wrist bone. Peel his arm way from your neck as you continue to press the Defender into his wrist.

Take him down to the ground. Continue to squeeze until you disarm the knife and escape.

HOME TRAINING EQUIPMENT

This is a water-based training dummy called Bob. Excellent for accuracy training.

Square focus pads are used to develop accuracy and power. Have someone hold it in different positions as you strike it from different angles.

Body Shields can be used to practice knee and kicking drills. Also, excellent for developing power in your elbow strikes.

Samuel Scott is available for lectures and seminars.

If you are interested in private or group training, please call us at 301-860-0030, or our toll free number, 1-866-860-0034.

For a copy of our Women's Personal Safety Instructional DVD, go to www.wps101.com.

Join our free Women's Personal Safety Network at www.thewpsn.com and click on community. This resourceful site is bringing women together from all over the world and all walks of life to help drastically reduce violence against women.

For more info on our Women's Personal Safety Network, email us at; info@thewpsn.com. Please share this site with all family, friends and co-workers to help bring an end to violence against women.

About the Author

Samuel Scott has been an advocate for Women's Safety for over 20 years. Born and raised in Long Island, New York, he began his martial arts training at age 12, strictly for self-defense.

Mr. Scott moved to Washington, DC to pursue a career in law enforcement. After working in the security field and private investigation, he gained employment with the Prince George's County Department of Corrections. This, Samuel Scott says, is where he received his greatest lesson about "the mindset and methods of the predator". For 15 years he received "awareness and avoidance" lessons straight from the horse's mouth. With this knowledge, along with countless hours of training and refining his personal safety program, he set out on an unstoppable mission to empower women all over the world.

Mr. Scott says "My first goal is to raise the level of awareness of the danger women face in this-increasingly violent society. Then encourage them to take action to avoid becoming a victim.

Below is an action list of what he's doing in the fight for women's safety:

- Founded Full Circle Martial Arts Academy in 1992.

- Formed a team of personal safety instructors that travel throughout the U.S. teaching "Personal Safety".

- In August and December, also known as "peak season" for predators, he hosts free workshops to help raise awareness during this dangerous time of the year.

- Developed a curriculum for a Personal Safety Keychain called "The Defender" and has taught hundreds of women how to use this simple, yet highly effective weapon.

- Hosts his own cable TV show, "The Self-defense Forum", where he shares his knowledge as well as invites other experts to share their knowledge in the field of personal safety.

- Developed training CD's on Women's Safety, and is currently developing a virtual "Online Training Program".

- Established a free online Women's Personal Safety Network to help keep women up to date with the latest crime waves, scams, sexual predators and other pertinent information. The goal is to bring women together from all over the world to help bring an end to violence against women.

Samuel Scott says, "We all have our calling. Helping people stay safe in a world that is plagued with violence is my calling...and I will follow my marching orders until my work is done!"

Abbreviated Biography of Samuel Scott

- Studied and trained in the martial arts for 30+ years

- Opened martial arts school in his basement in 1992 (Currently the Proprietor of three schools.)

- Holds "Instructor" ranking in five different martial arts

- Inducted into the Blackbelt Hall of Fame

- Founder of Self-defense System – "Talahib Kuntao" and has received International recognition from the "World Head Sokeship Council"

- Received a proclamation from Prince George's County Maryland's County Executive for Outstanding Community Service

- Received "Master Instructor" rank in 1997

- Instructs defensive tactics program to Law Enforcement/Federal Agents both domestic and abroad

- Featured on Channel 9 News, Washington, D.C.

- Co-founder of "Safe Passage", an Executive Protection company that provides personal protection for VIP's throughout the world.

- Featured in various news mediums – Gazette, Prince George's Journal, Fox 5 News, Afro-American, BET Heart & Soul

- Host of award-winning cable program, titled "The Self-Defense Forum"

- Graduate of Executive Protection Institute (Virginia)

BOOK COVER ANSWERS

Seven (7) things that are wrong with the cover scenario.

1. She allowed him to invade her space.

2. She took her eyes off him.

3. She didn't bring her watch up to eye level in order to observe him while she gives him the time.

4. She didn't step back with one foot for balance.

5. She has her bag strapped across her neck.

6. She's smiling at the stranger.

7. She doesn't have a personal safety device in her hand for protection.

These 7 mistakes give the predator the green light to make you his next victim. Read this book and learn how to avoid fitting the victim profile.